POCKET PICTORIAL

The
Peak District

Simon Kirwan

MYRIAD
LONDON

Buxton The Old Hall Hotel (above) occupies the site of the former townhouse of Bess of Hardwick and her husband the Earl of Shrewsbury. Mary Queen of Scots was held here as a prisoner in 1573.

Devonshire Royal Hospital Originally a stable block (left) it is now part of the University of Derby.

Pavilion Gardens This set of beautiful Victorian buildings (above right) includes the Octagon and the Paxton Suite.

The Crescent Modelled on the Royal Crescent at Bath.

Bakewell A busy market town and unofficial capital of the eastern Peaks, Bakewell was developed in the early 19th century by the Duke of Rutland, one of whose country seats was nearby Haddon Hall. The duke wanted to turn Bakewell into a spa to rival Buxton, established by the Duke of Devonshire. The imposing Norman church of All Saints (left) contains a monument to Sir John Manners and his wife of Haddon Hall. The famous Bakewell pudding and its close cousin the Bakewell tart (right) originated in this town. The historic Holme Bridge (below and below right) dates from 1664 and spans the river Wye at Bakewell. Originally a packhorse bridge, it was built here close to a ford which had long been used as a crossing by wool drovers and merchants.

Ashford-in-the-Water A quiet and idyllic village, Ashford is most famous for the so-called black marble, an impure form of limestone which turns black when polished. First quarried in 1748 by Henry Watson, it was much loved by the Victorians who used it in the production of fireplaces, vases and jewellery. Some fine examples of black marble can be seen in the great limestone church of the Holy Trinity (left). Largely rebuilt in 1871, the base of the church tower dates from the 13th century. The church has a fine black marble table as well as a plaque to the memory of Henry Watson.

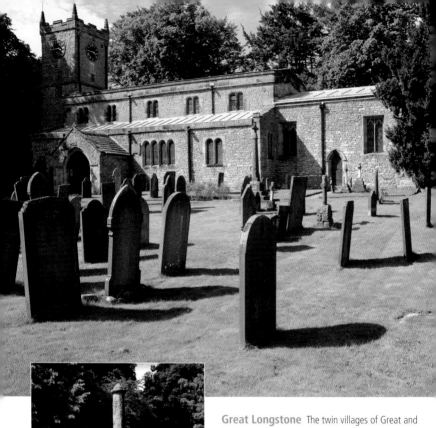

Great Longstone The twin villages of Great and Little Longstone sit beneath Longstone Edge just east of Hassop. Longstone Edge is now disfigured by the lead workings which brought the village its early prosperity. The medieval cross (left) dates even further back to the time when Great Longstone had a flourishing weaving and shoemaking industry, whose patron saint Crispin is commemorated in the adjacent Crispin Inn. St Giles' church (above), hidden away at the end of the village, dates back to the end of the 13th century. Inside there is a memorial to Dr Edward Buxton who, in the early part of the 19th century, tended the village during an outbreak of typhus.

Hassop Three miles north of the market town of Bakewell, the tiny village of Hassop grew up around the local leadmining industry. The imposing Hassop Hall (below) was rebuilt on the site of a much older house owned by the Eyre family, whose wealth came from leadmining. An old leadmine still exists under the house beneath a man-hole hidden in the cellar. The church of All Saints (right) was designed as a pri-vate chapel for the Eyre family in 1818. It is connected to the house by an underground passage. Hassop station, to the south of the village, was built in 1863 to serve the Duke of Devonshire at Chatsworth House.

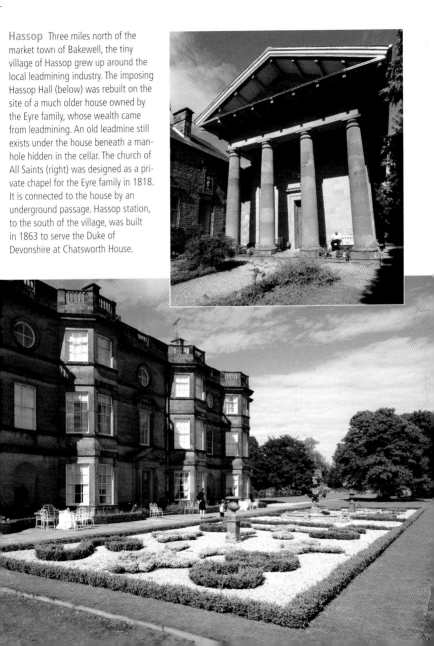

Tideswell The magnificent 14th-century church of St John the Baptist (left) is often called "the Cathedral of the Peak" and is a testament to the wealth of the area in the Middle Ages. The church was built by Sir John Foljambe, a member of the well-known Derbyshire landowning family, and has a beautiful high nave and outstanding carvings by local woodcarvers the Hunstones.

Litton These 17th and 18th-century stone cottages (right and right below) are clustered around the village green with its stocks and ancient cross in front of the Red Lion pub. Litton flourished as a centre of stocking-making in the 18th century. Litton Mill, built in 1762, is now a ruin and stands as a monument to the many orphans who toiled here in appalling conditions.

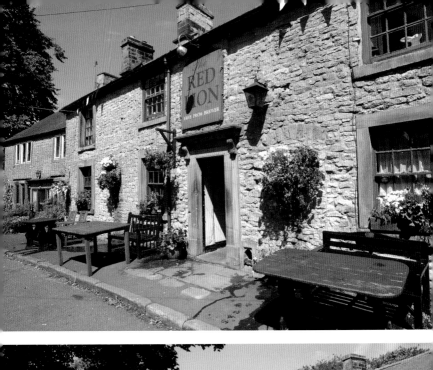

Chelmorton Four miles south-east of Buxton, the village of Chelmorton is 1200ft (366m) above sea level, the highest settlement in Derbyshire. The steep hill of Chelmorton Low looms above the village from which a stream flows down bearing the name of Illy Willy Water. Parts of the church of St John the Baptist (right) date back to Norman times, although the spire was added to the tower in

the 15th century. Chelmorton retains many medieval strip farms in the fields around the village, and some of the 13 surviving strips are visible to this day. Most strip-farming of this type has long since disappeared to make way for modern agriculture with its much larger fields. However, the land in Chelmorton was considered to be of such poor quality that the medieval field pattern remained untouched up to the present day.

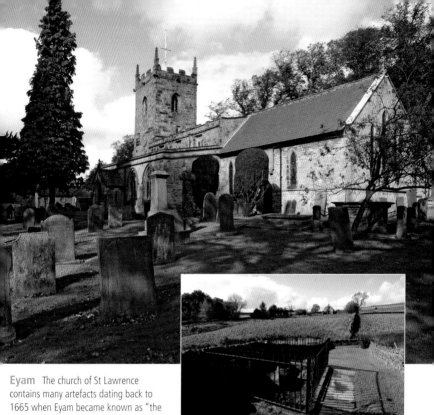

Eyam The church of St Lawrence contains many artefacts dating back to 1665 when Eyam became known as "the plague village", when a travelling tailor carried the plague to the village from London in a parcel of flea-infested cloth. The village rector, William Mompesson, persuaded the inhabitants to quarantine the area in order to prevent the plague spreading to neighbouring villages. The churchyard of St Lawrence is the resting place for many of the plague victims. Among those buried here is William Mompesson's wife, Catherine. Eyam Hall (right) is a 17th-century manor house, home of the Wright family.

Monsal Dale In the 19th century, this beautiful area was thought to have been ruined by the arrival of the railway. Now it is one of the most highly regarded beauty spots in the Peaks. Pictured above is the viaduct which carried the Midland Railway over the river Wye with the view from the viaduct (left).

Upperdale The tiny hamlet of Upperdale with the river Wye at its centre is situated amidst some of the finest limestone scenery in the Peak District.

Chatsworth Often referred to as "the Palace of the Peaks", Chatsworth is one of the most magnificent stately homes in Britain. The house is largely the creation of the first Duke of Devonshire. Between 1686-1707 he remodelled the original house, built by the formidable Bess of Hardwick and her second husband William Cavendish, and turned it into a fabulous Palladian mansion. The gardens were designed by Lancelot "Capability" Brown who swept away the formal gardens and created today's open natural loooking landscape. Below is the grand Stable Block at Chatsworth.

Formal gardens

Whilst Capability Brown created the "natural" parkland setting of Chatsworth, it was Joseph Paxton who designed the gardens close to the house and incorporated a number of existing features, such as the Seahorse Fountain (right) and the Cascade (below right). Between 1836-41 Paxton built an amazing iron-framed conservatory at Chatsworth. This giant structure, the largest glass building in the world at the time, was demolished in 1920. One of the most popular features at Chatsworth is the Cascade. To the west of the house, this is a set of 24 stone steps over which water flows from a group of fountains.

Haddon Hall The romantic and mysterious Haddon Hall is situated next to the river Wye just south of Bakewell. It is one of the finest medieval and Tudor houses in England and has been the home of the Manners family, the Dukes of Rutland, since 1567. The air of romance that lingers around the house is in part due to the legend that in 1558 Lady Dorothy Vernon eloped from the house on horseback with Sir John Manners. This inspired the 1927 film *Dorothy Vernon of Haddon Hall*, starring Mary Pickford. Today Haddon Hall is famous for its gardens and its terraced rose plantings are a great favourite with visitors.

Curbar Edge The imposing edges fringing the Peak District are at their most spectacular north of Bakewell where Froggatt's Edge, Curbar Edge and Baslow Edge join in a breathtaking sequence overlooking the valley of the river Derwent and the villages of Curbar and Calver.

Matlock The town of Matlock (above) is dominated by the vast Hydro building, a former spa built in 1853, by businessman John Smedley. He saw the potential of Matlock and nearby Matlock Bath as a hydro to rival other British and Continental towns, where ailing Victorians would come to "take the waters". The setting of Matlock Bath (left) is distinctly alpine, with steep and wooded valleys stretching up from the valley bottom. The Pump Room and the Matlock Pavilion in Matlock Bath (right) were surrounded by hotels in the Victorian and Edwardian era. The domed Royal Pavilion at the centre of the Spa complex was constructed in 1910; it is now the Peak District Mining Museum.

Cromford Mill Constructed by Sir Richard Arkwright in 1783 this is now at the centre of the Derwent Valley Mills World Heritage Site, which also includes Smedley's Mill at Lea Bridge and the Silk Mill at Derby.

Heights of Abraham The cable car carries visitors up the incline of the wooded gorge to the Heights of Abraham above Matlock Bath.

Black Rock An outcrop of gritstone sculpted by the wind and rain, Black Rock hangs high above the historic town of Cromford.

Ilam Hall The distinctive alpine-style village of Ilam at the lower end of the river Manifold, was built by industrialist Jesse Watts-Russell. The original village once stood near Ilam Hall (above) a Victorian Gothic mansion surrounded by open park and woodland. Walks stretch down to the river in the valley below and open up panoramic views across Dovedale.

Dovedale The spectacular limestone scenery of Dovedale (left, below and overleaf) with its steep-sided valleys and exposed crags is a favourite with visitors to the south Peaks.

Thorpe Cloud Hill The conical summit of Thorpe Cloud Hill (left) is one of the most distinctive sights in Dovedale. The peak towers above the village of Thorpe at the southern entrance to Dovedale where the river Dove flows from Dovedale into Lindale.

Ashbourne Situated at the southern tip of Derbyshire, Ashbourne is an attractive market town. The splendid stone building in Church Street (below) housed the original Queen Elizabeth Grammar School, established in 1585. The Royal Shrovetide football game is contested between the two sides of the town.

Ramshaw The "fingerstone" is part of the Ramshaw Rocks which lie between the two farming hamlets of Upper and Lower Elkstone on the edge of the western Peaks.

The Roaches The weirdly-shaped rocks of the Roaches form one of the most impressive and dramatic outcrops of the Western Peaks and provide a challenge to climbers. Many classic routes have been established and some of these have been given colourful names such as "Valkyrie", "the Sloth" and "the Swan". On reaching the summit there are spectacular views of Tittesworth Reservoir and the town of Leek in Staffordshire. Hen Cloud (above) is a separate southern extremity of the Roaches and overlooks the hamlet of Upper Hulme.

Castleton Situated at the western end of the broad Hope Valley, where the dark gritstone Peaks of the north give way to the white limestone Peaks of the south, the picturesque village of Castleton is one of the most popular destinations in the Peak District. At the heart of the village is the square with its unusual Celtic cross. Peveril Castle (left) is perched high above Cavedale, overlooking Castleton. The castle was built in 1080 by William Peverel, one of William the Conqueror's trusted allies. The sheer sides of Cavedale made the castle impregnable; its role was to defend the royal hunting grounds and the local leadmining industry.

Mam Tor Known as the "Mother Mountain" because of its softly rounded contours, Mam Tor is formed from an unstable mix of sandstone and shale. The entire hill is gradually slipping into the valley giving the peak its other name of the "shivering mountain". From Castleton there is an enjoyable 6.5 mile (10km) walk (right) that takes in Lose Hill and Winnats Pass. The walk goes full circle with breathtaking views of Mam Tor and Peveril Castle before returning to Castleton.

The Pennine Way Britain's first long-distance footpath, seen here close to its start at the little village of Edale (above). By tradition, the last stop before embarking on the walk is to call at the Old Nags Head pub in the village. The path continues for 250 miles northwards to its finish at Kirk Yetholm on the Scottish border. From Edale the Pennine Way winds through Grindsbrook Clough before climbing to Kinder Scout, the highest point in Derbyshire.

Old Glossop Situated in the far north-west of Derbyshire, just outside the boundaries of the Peak District National Park, Glossop and its neigbour Old Glossop (above) expanded rapidly as the wool and cotton industries grew; many of the old cottages gathered around the parish church in Old Glossop would have been occupied by weavers and their weaving frames.

Chapel-en-le-Frith The busy market town of Chapel-en-le-Frith (left) stands 776ft (237m) above sea level between Stockport and Buxton. Church Brow is a steep, cobbled street leading down from Market Street to the High Street, lined with quaint stone cottages. The Peak Forest Tramway once passed through the town and linked Bugsworth Canal Basin, at the head of the Peak Forest Canal, to the limestone quarries at Dove Holes Dale.

Kinder The windswept 15-mile wide plateau of Kinder Scout is a desolate mix of wind and ice-shattered boulders, peat bogs and deep trenches called "groughs". Kinder Downfall (bottom) is on the north-western edge of Kinder Scout where much of the plateau's water gathers to drop 98ft (30m) on to the land below.

Stanage Edge Lying on the western moors with views over the Derwent valley, Stanage Edge is the largest and most impressive of the Peaks' gritstone edges and is visible from far down in the Hope Valley below. The entire edge is approximately 3.5 miles long from its northern tip to the southern point near the Cowper Stone. It is an ideal spot for climbing and is within easy reach of Sheffield. A paved packhorse route ran along the top of Stanage Edge and its path can still be traced.

Over Owler Tor The surreal landscape of Over Owler Tor (right) and Higger Tor is located south-east of Hathersage. This landscape is thought to have been the inspiration for Charlotte Brontë's *Jane Eyre*.

Higger Tor Just beyond the rocks of Higger Tor is the remarkable escarpment hill fort of Carl Wark. This formidable earthwork utilised the sheer cliffs on three sides to provide an easily defended position.